# Finding History: Twenty-One Tales of Tacoma's Temple Beth El

Written by Deb Freedman

"In Jewish history there are no coincidences."
Elie Wiesel

"Not all treasure is silver and gold, mate."
Capt. Jack Sparrow (Johnny Depp), Pirates of the Caribbean

Acknowledgments

The author wishes to thank the Temple Beth El staff and clergy for their support and expertise, Andy Mauer for tracking down archival records before her retirement, the many Temple members who provided history and memories, and the women of Sisterhood for their tireless good cheer. Deep appreciation goes to Harold Friedman for his editing assistance and profound friendship.



Imprint: Independently published

ISBN: 9798300539276

Library of Congress Control Number:
2024925901

**Cover image:** Southwest corner of Temple Beth El, Tacoma, Washington.

# Introduction

Temple Beth El is a Jewish congregation located in Tacoma, Washington. The current building was designed with architectural features that symbolize elements of the history of the Jewish people, in collaboration with the late Rabbi Richard Rosenthal. The Temple also displays artwork made by members and several artifacts from earlier Jewish congregations in Tacoma.

The Twenty-One Tales series began in 2008 as a grant-funded local history supplement for area schools, through Tacoma Historical Society. Rabbi Bruce Kadden subsequently suggested a book on the art and architecture of Temple Beth El. This work combines elements of both.

It is written as a treasure hunt. Whether the twenty-one following items are discovered in person or experienced via the printed page, together they tell tales of a vibrant Jewish community spanning more than one hundred and thirty years.

## 1. **1893 Window into History**

Find the large wooden window frame with a colored glass Star of David.

This framed window stands on display in the conversation nook, below the ramp connecting the rotunda and the main foyer. The window was originally above the front entry of Tacoma's first Temple building, dedicated at South $10^{th}$ and I Streets in the fall of 1893.

The Tacoma area's earliest known Jewish families lived in Steilacoom in the 1850s and along the Tacoma waterfront in the 1870s. By the 1880s Tacoma had several Jewish social clubs and a thriving Jewish merchant district along the main thoroughfare, Pacific Avenue. The Jewish community rented lodge rooms for High Holy Days and in 1888 formed a benevolent society and developed a cemetery.

Tacoma's Jewish women formed the Lady Judith Montefiore Society in 1890 and took the lead in organizing a religious school. They were assisted by Rabbi Jacob Bloch, from Portland's Congregation Beth Israel. When Tacoma's first Jewish Reform congregation was incorporated in 1892, members also took the name Congregation Beth Israel.

However, while the first Temple building was under construction in 1893, there was a nationwide economic disaster. Over the next decade many of Tacoma's Jewish merchants left the city. The congregation lost more traditional members in 1912 after changing their by-laws to read "The services in Temple Beth Israel shall be of strict Reform with Union Prayer Book ... and no hats shall be worn by any male person attending services and the Trustees are hereby empowered to enforce the new by-law."

In 1918 the congregation sold the building on the corner of South 10th and I Streets to members of the First Seventh Day Adventists church and the Moorish domes were removed.

Fifty years later the church was torn down to develop the lot for parking. The new owners salvaged several artifacts. In 2008 Larry and Mardie Nicholson donated the framed colored glass window to Temple Beth El, along with an original hanging light and chain and a wooden stair newel post.

## 2. **1899 Marriage of Founding Families**

Find the personalized encyclopedia set with a special anniversary bookplate.

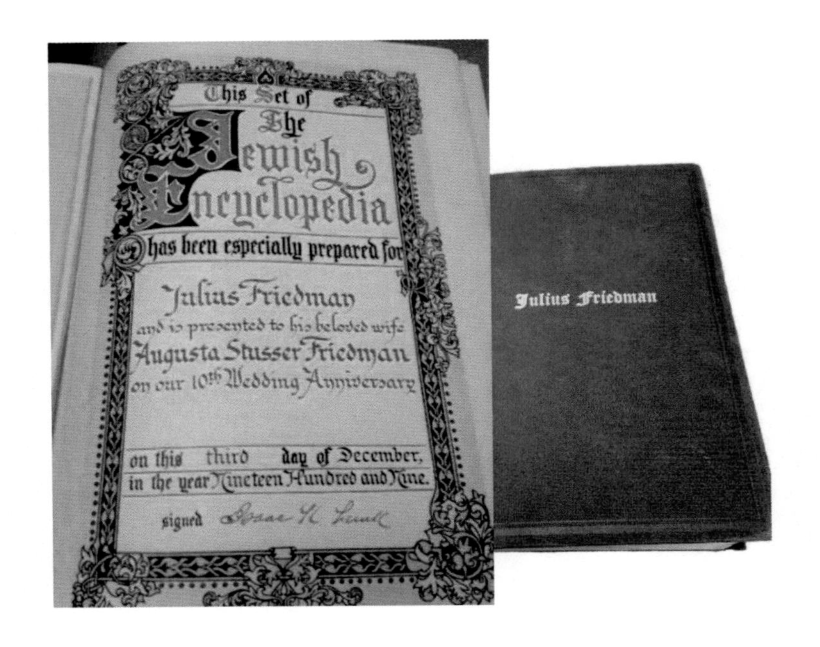


This 1909 edition of the Jewish Encyclopedia is now in the reference section of the Temple's library. The 12-volume set was purchased for Julius Friedman by his wife, Augusta (Stusser) Friedman, as a gift for their tenth anniversary. Their 1899 marriage united two large founding families of Tacoma's Orthodox Jewish community.

While many of Tacoma's pioneer Jews had roots in central Europe, a cluster of families had begun emigrating from the Courland region of what is now Latvia. They spoke Yiddish and came together for daily prayer minyans. In the fall of 1892, the "Hebrew Orthodox of Tacoma" publicly announced separate High Holy Day services. Tacoma's Jewish population had grown large enough to openly divide and would remain so for nearly seventy years.

ARTICLES OF INCORPORATION

—OF—

Chevra Talmud Torah

This is to Certify, That on the 15th day of December 1908 Philip B. Friedman, Max Zuckerkorn, Samuel Friedman, Joe Sussman, Nathan Friedman, Chas Stusser, Julius Friedman, Ike Moses, M Jacobson and H. Stusser and R. Winkleman

at the town or city of Tacoma in Pierce county, State of Washington, entered into an agreement in writing, duly subscribed by them and each of them, of which the following is a true copy:

AGREEMENT TO INCORPORATE

This Agreement, Made this 15th day of December A.D. 1908

Witnesseth:

FIRST, That we, the undersigned Philip B. Friedman, Max Zuckerkorn, Samuel Friedman, Joe Sussman, Nathan Friedman, Chas. Stusser, Julius Friedman, Ike Moses, M. Jacobson and H. Stusser and R. Winkleman

subscribers hereto, have associated and do hereby associate ourselves for the purpose and with the intention of forming a corporation under the provisions of an act of the legislature of the State of Washington, entitled "An act to provide for the incorporation of associations for social, charitable and educational purposes, approved by the Governor of Washington on the 21st day of March, 1895."

SECOND, The name of the said corporation shall be Chevra Talmud Torah

Tacoma's Latvian Orthodox Jews formally organized as Chevra Talmud Torah in 1906, hired kosher butcher Rabbi Meier Elyn in 1907, and incorporated in 1908. The incorporation documents clearly noted that "Under no circumstances will any man or boy be allowed in place of worship with head uncovered." After incorporation the congregation purchased and renovated a church building at 1529 Tacoma Avenue South. It was their place of worship, their *Shul*, for the next 15 years.

## 3. **1912 Tale of a Torah**

Find the tall Torah with a special inscription on the top wooden circles.

This Torah holds a place of honor in the ark of Temple Beth El. It is the largest of the Torahs and has distinctive decorative handles. Around the wooden discs at the top are celluloid insets with Hebrew characters. The words Tacoma and Washington are spelled out phonetically, along with abbreviations representing the Hebrew year corresponding to 1912. By turning the Torah and completing the circle, the entire Yiddish phrase reads "Chevrah Ahavas Israel Tacoma Washington 5673." The name means a close-knit society of friends with love and solidarity for all Jews. The Torah was commissioned by members of an emerging congregation that until recently had been lost to history.

The late 1890s and early 1900s brought many Jewish families to Tacoma not only from Latvia, but also from Russian-controlled Poland. They adapted to the poor economy by gathering scrap metal and selling second-hand and pawned merchandise. In 1912 several of these Polish families formed a separate Orthodox congregation, Chevrah Ahavas Israel, and held their own fall Holy Day services. They commissioned a new Torah and held a Torah dedication ceremony in January of 1913.

Officers and trustees filed articles of incorporation in the fall of 1913. The next summer they organized their own Jewish cemetery, named Chevra Kadisha, and purchased land adjoining the existing Jewish Cemetery, Home of Peace.

1914 also brought worsening conditions in Europe. The threat of war added to the challenges of Tacoma's divided Jewish community. Chevrah Ahavas Israel likely never existed for more than several years. Some members moved elsewhere, while the majority returned to Tacoma's two other Jewish congregations.

Over time, the history of Chevrah Ahavas Israel was lost and blurred into that of Chevra Talmud Torah. The 1912 date on this Torah handle possibly led to the mistaken belief that Chevra Talmud Torah was founded in 1912. That error was reinforced when it was included in a timeline of Jewish history, set in stone tiles along the exterior entrance wall of Temple Beth El.

*Correction: founded 1906, incorporated 1908*

## 4. **1922 Memorial Windows**

Find the large, framed photograph of nine memorial windows.

This framed arrangement of photos of memorial windows is displayed on the north wall of the main foyer. The windows are from the second Temple Beth Israel, built in 1922, and feature Jewish symbols within Pacific Northwest settings. The photos were taken in 2001 by congregant Jeff Freedman.

Tacoma's economy was greatly boosted by the impact of the First World War, including the development of Fort Lewis, the Port of Tacoma, and a spurt of shipbuilding. Many of Tacoma's Jewish families prospered and moved to Tacoma's North End.

The first Temple building, which lacked central heating and a modern kitchen, was sold in 1918. In 1919 the congregation purchased two building lots on the corner of North 4$^{th}$ and J Streets. Religious school was held in rented rooms in Triangle Hall while the trustees raised building funds. They also revised the constitution and by-laws to change their name to Reform Congregation Beth Israel.

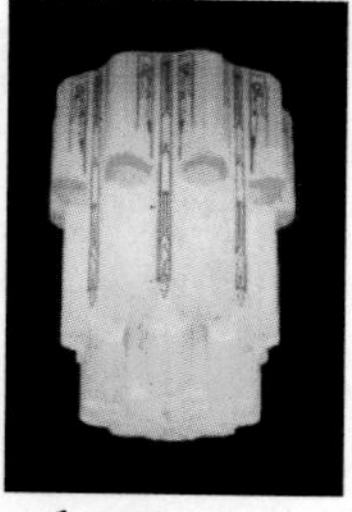

The congregation raised money through a combination of donations and contributions from members, but still needed a $12,000 bank loan. Morris Kleiner donated lumber, Lewis Brothers provided nine chandeliers, and Harold Davis gave an insurance policy.

The congregation already had funds from the estate of millionaire hops broker Herman Klaber, who had died in 1912 in the sinking of the *Titanic.* Klaber's will provided for a window to honor the memory of his parents. Sam Andrews pledged two more windows in remembrance of his late wife and her parents, and others followed suit.

Building construction began in the spring of 1922 and the congregation placed historic documents in the cornerstone. The building was dedicated on September 27, 1922. Over the next few years other families donated additional memorial windows, with added ventilation. *(See complete list of names and donors on pages 50-51.)*

The congregation stayed in this building for over forty years, despite challenges of leaking walls, furnace failures, and limited classroom space and parking. The women of the Temple Sisterhood led campaigns to renovate the kitchen, replace the organ, and create a library. As a direct result of the post-World War II baby boom the congregation purchased a small house adjoining the property and used it for more classrooms and office space.

## 5. **1925 Concrete Lintels**

Find the rounded concrete lintels with grape vines and the Ten Commandments.

This pair of concrete lintels is displayed in the courtyard outside the social hall. The architectural sections were originally above the main entrance of the second Talmud Torah, built in 1925 at South 4th and I Streets. The artifacts were salvaged by Dorothy Grenley when the building was demolished in 1968. They were donated to Temple Beth El in 2006, after nearly forty years in storage. An anonymous donor provided a granite base and inscription.

The members of Chevra Talmud Torah had also prospered as Tacoma's economy improved during the first World War and many had moved north as well. Since proximity to the *Shul* was essential for Orthodox worshipers, the congregation purchased three building lots in the spring of 1924, on the west side of Wright Park.

Construction began in early 1925, through the same firm that had built Temple Beth Israel. The architectural plans were adapted to include a school room at the west end and a pillared stone entrance. The building was clad in brick rather than stucco and featured a curved sanctuary ceiling twinkling with painted gold stars.

Signage installed on the east end of the building identified it as Talmud Torah Synagogue. The congregation was no longer simply a Chevra.

Again, the women of the congregation lent their support. For many decades they held annual rummage sales through the Women's Auxiliary and prepared countless meals in the synagogue's kosher kitchen. Many held leadership roles in the Council of Jewish Women and Hadassah.

The synagogue basement included a stage that was the backdrop for a wide variety of activities. Members of the Young Hebrew Moderates were active in Tacoma's intramural sports leagues. The girls of the Jewish Juniors sponsored card parties and dances and helped teach in the religious school. The congregation held a re-dedication event in 1930 and in 1935 paid off its ten-year mortgage.

## 6. **1945 Name Change**

Find the bronze sign with a geographic name from a mountain and peninsula in Egypt.

This memorial tablet was originally at Talmud Torah Synagogue, later renamed Sinai Temple. It is on the wall in the hallway between the Sanctuary and the Chapel, along with similar signage from Reform Temple Beth Israel. The individual names on the tablets remember deceased relatives and recognizes their date of death, or *yahrzeit.*

In 1936 the members of Talmud Torah chose Rabbi Baruch Treiger to lead them. Under his direction the congregation moved to a Conservative style of worship, continuing many traditions but increasing the role of women and adding Confirmation for teens.

As worldwide anti-Semitism increased, Rabbi Treiger began hosting an annual city-wide non-sectarian lecture series. Over a span of five years the series drew more than 4,000 people, providing an opportunity for non-Jews to interact with Jews in a positive manner.

During the Forties the congregation was led by Rabbi Julius DeKoven, Rabbi Solomon Herbst, and Rabbi Leo Trepp. In the fall of 1945 as Americans tried to grasp the enormity of the humanitarian crisis in Europe, Jews around the world prayed for a Jewish homeland. In October of 1945 the members of Talmud Torah showed their support by taking the name Sinai Temple.

In May of 1948 the congregation celebrated 40 years since its incorporation. That same week Jews around the world celebrated the creation of the State of Israel.

## 7. **1960 Certificate of Union**

Find the framed certificate recognizing when Temple Beth El became a congregation.

לכה ונועצה יחדו׃

The Union of American Hebrew Congregations

Temple Beth El

Tacoma, Washington

This certificate dated June 5, 1960, welcomed a new congregation, Temple Beth El, to membership in the Union of American Hebrew Congregations, now the Union for Reform Judaism. The new congregation was a result of a historic merger of the two existing congregations: Temple Beth Israel and Sinai Temple. The certificate is displayed on the north wall of the main foyer, along with photos of both Temples.

By the 1950s, many of Tacoma's Jewish families from both congregations found that they had more in common than they had differences. They had lived through two horrific World Wars and a financial Depression. They were mostly born in the United States, and many had been in Tacoma for several generations. They also had worked together in Jewish organizations such as B'nai B'rith, Hadassah, the Council of Jewish Women, and several European relief and immigrant aid organizations. Their local Jewish organizations regularly worked together on Israel Bond campaigns. Most importantly, their children went to public school together.

At the same time, Temple Beth Israel had only about 90 families and congregational finances were a continual challenge. Sinai Temple had more clergy changes than in the past. A rabbinic opening in 1959 created an opportunity.

By October 1959 both congregations had given fact-finding committee members authority to work together to effect a merger of the two congregations. Committees presented a draft constitution in March 1960, by-laws and budgets in April, and candidates for board positions in May.

The final vote on June 5, 1960, reflected a long process of compromise. Section one of the "Religious Practices" portion of the new constitution stated that "wearing of Yamalka and Tallis shall be optional with the individual member." Section two prohibited serving pork and shellfish products; or meat and dairy at the same time. Section three guaranteed that "The Congregation shall provide facilities for traditional services for those members desiring them." Section four provided that the choir was to be entirely of Jewish members, if feasible.

In May the committees had also begun soliciting names for the new congregation. Members mailed in cards with their votes, and chose the name Temple Beth El, a house of God.

## 8. **Four Decades of Leadership**

Find the portrait of a seated Rabbi who led the congregation for over forty years.

This portrait of Rabbi Richard Rosenthal, *z"l, (*of blessed memory) is displayed in the main foyer on the wall between the Chapel and the Judaica Shop. Below rests a journal of memorials from congregants after his passing. Rabbi Rosenthal was ideally suited to facilitate the merger and to lead the united congregations.

Richard Rosenthal witnessed Kristallnacht, the Night of Broken Glass, as a nine-year-old child in Germany. His father was beaten nearly beyond recognition. With the help of the Jewish Resettlement Agency, he, his sister and his parents, were able to emigrate to London. They subsequently moved to New York, then to Shreveport, Louisiana, in April of 1940. He related that he didn't really feel comfortable in either the Orthodox or Reform congregations there and moved back and forth between the two.

Rabbi Rosenthal was ordained at Hebrew Union College in 1954 and served two years as an Army Chaplain before coming to Tacoma in August 1956 to lead Temple Beth Israel. The following year he taught a series of home-study classes on the subject of "Decisive Moments in Jewish History," a theme that a decade later contributed to a dramatic architectural feature.

In the fall of 1959 Rabbi Rosenthal led Friday night services at Reform Temple Beth Israel. As Sinai Temple was temporarily without a rabbi, he also assisted with Conservative services at Sinai Temple on Saturday mornings. His ability to move between the two congregations has been credited by many as a key factor in achieving the 1960 merger.

The combined congregations worshipped together at 1960 Rosh Hashanah services in the Beth Israel Building, *(below left)* renamed North Temple Beth El. Sinai Temple *(below right)* was renamed the South Temple and housed the Temple offices and religious school.

In the spring of 1964, the congregation sold the North Temple building to an Apostolic Faith Church. All activities were at South 4th and I Streets for four years, while the congregation prepared to build a new Jewish home in Tacoma's growing West End. Rabbi Rosenthal worked closely with architects and artists and provided key Jewish themes for the new building.

## 9. **1967 Inspiration**

Find the architect's 3-D model of a unique building design.

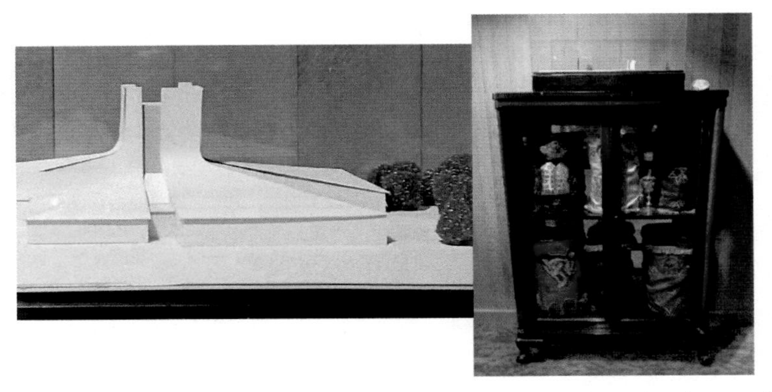

This architect's model reflects the inspiration of the architectural firm of Robert Billsbrough Price and Partners. The model is on display in the northeast corner of the main foyer, above a cabinet exhibiting historical Torah covers.

As Tacoma's neighborhood demographics shifted, the congregation again looked south, but also west. Realtor Victor Lyon chaired the building committee and secured lots across from the newly opened Tacoma Community College. A dedicated campaign team went to work soliciting contributions.

**Our Campaign Organization**

| | |
|---|---|
| Rabbi | Richard Rosenthal |
| President | Dr. Kurt Blau |
| Committee Chairmen | |
| Major Gifts | Walter Etsekson |
| General Gifts | Jerry Spellman |
| Publications | M. Harvey Segall |
| Hostesses | Mrs. Leo Sarkowsky |
| Arrangements | Mrs. Saul Levy |
| | Mrs. Herman Lehrer |
| Pledge Counseling | William Sherman |
| Follow-Up | Dr. Haskel Maier |
| Building Committee Chairman | Victor Lyon |
| Campaign Chairman | Bernard Friedman |
| Campaign Treasurer | Favius E. Witenberg |
| Secretary-Recorder | Mrs. Kurt Blau |
| Captains | Martin Brasham |
| | Henry W. Callin |
| | Jay Grenley |
| | Harrold Jaffe |
| | Herman Kleiner |
| | Jack Zidell |

Members of the extended Kleiner family were among the many who posed for photos at the groundbreaking ceremony on April 23, 1967.

The Rome Company completed construction in time for dedication over the weekend of May 17-19, 1968. The building's sweeping rooflines intentionally recalled the outstretched tents that were the Israelites' first homes while wandering in the desert during the Exodus. The interior rooflines of the Sanctuary are equally dramatic.

## 10. **Towering Alphabet**

Find the Hebrew alphabet letters between towering flames of glass.

These ascending and descending Hebrew letters are flanked by columns of glass. Together they tower above the main foyer. The glass flames represent the pillar of fire that led the Jewish ancestors in their wanderings. Exodus 13:21: "Adonai went before them in a pillar of cloud by day, to guide them along the way, and in a pillar of fire, by night, that they might travel day and night."

The glasswork panels in the tower were fabricated by the Cummings Studio of Pinedale, California. The Studio was purchased in 1921 by Harold William Cummings (1897-1962) and continued after his death by his sons. The firm's chief designer during the Fifties and Sixties was Hilda Dresel Sachs (1910-1996). On summer evenings, sunlight coming through the windows creates colorful reflections throughout the lobby below.

The carvings of the Hebrew alphabet are also symbolic. The 1968 Temple dedication booklet noted that they serve as a reminder of how the "Torah brings us to God even as God is brought into our lives." A 1981 visitor's guide described them as "carvings of the Hebrew alphabet, flying upward. The Torah serves as a ladder by which Jews ascend to God and by which God makes his will known to us."

The Hebrew alphabet carvings and numerous other panels throughout the Temple were designed and fabricated by Harold Balazs (1928-2017). Temple Beth El selected him to create the carvings early in his career, before he became a prominent public and liturgical artist and sculptor.

During a later visit to Tacoma, Mr. Balazs discussed his technique for the project. Since he was working within a limited budget, he purchased a large quantity of Georgia Sugar Pine at a bargain price. Mr. Balazs said he stained and preserved the wood by sealing it with melted paraffin. He gave many of the designs metal inserts, secured with boat nails. Mr. Balazs created the artwork on modular panels, which he assembled in his studio near Spokane and brought to Tacoma for installation.

## 11. **Holocaust Drawing**

Find the child's drawing of families on a railroad car.

These images show railroad cars going to the WWII death camps, as viewed through the mind and hand of a little child. They are based on pictures found in a concentration camp after the war and are located at the bottom of the Holocaust Memorial in the southwest corner of the main foyer.

The panel on the right contains the words of the martyrology from the Day of Atonement service. Written originally to remember the martyrs in Roman times, it serves as a memorial prayer for the six million Jews who died in Europe's concentration camps. The left panel bears the words of Joel 2:28 within two tablets. The symbols and figures across the top of the panels speak of the continuity of family life, reminders of Jewish hope for renewal. Together the panels span the reverse sides of the Ark in the Sanctuary.

Two walls in the foyer support art installations of the *Etz Chayim,* the Tree of Life. The tree outside the Chapel has leaves, stones, and acorns inscribed with names and dates honoring achievements, events, and contributions to Temple Beth El.

The tree on the south wall was a 1975 gift from Anna Grinspan Mandles (1886-1976) "in appreciation of the generous gifts which enhance the beauty of our temple." The forty-two memorials inscribed on each leaf reflect contributions made mostly between 1968 and 1986. The donations supported major elements such as sanctuary and religious school furniture, doors, and glass windows.

A bronze *yahrzeit* tablet on the east wall of the foyer remembers Anna's husband, Henry Mandles (1878-1950). It was originally used at Temple Beth Israel to display the weekly *yahrzeit* names.

## 12. **Highest Word**

Find the carving of the Hebrew pronoun that begins the Ten Commandments.

High atop the front of the Sanctuary, nearly touching the ceiling, are twin panels bearing the Hebrew word *Anochi.* They recall the first word of the Ten Commandments, *(Exodus 20:2)* "I am the Lord your God."

Far below them, beneath the Ark doors, are twin panels with the last word of the Ten Commandments, *"l're-echa,"* your neighbor. The ten blocks in between have been compared to a totem pole, graphically telling our people's history. Each panel represents a major theme in the development of Torah and Judaism. The panel numbers begin at the bottom and ascend, starting with the Ten Commandments.

**Panel 1:**
**Ten Commandments**

Exodus and accepting the Torah at Sinai

**Panel 2:**
**Biblical Tradition**

Institutions and values of Jewish life, priestly hands raised in blessing

**Panel 3:**
**Rabbinic Tradition**

Rabbinical literature, study of Talmud and Torah

**Panel 4:**
**Judaism Meets Philosophy**

Influence of Greek and Roman

**Panel 5:**
**The Golden Age of Spain**

Poetry and song represented by David's Harp

**Panel 6:**
**Mystical Tradition**

Mystic tradition expressed in the Zohar

**Panel 7:**
**Eastern European Traditions**

Hasidic tradition: wisdom, insight and knowledge

**Panel 8:**
**Western Europe**

French enlightenment period ended by Hitler

**Panel 9:**
**Zionist Tradition**

Israel,
Theodore Herzl,
*Im Tirtzu*

**Panel 10:**
**America**

Jeremiah's
reminder to the
exiles to seek the
peace of the city

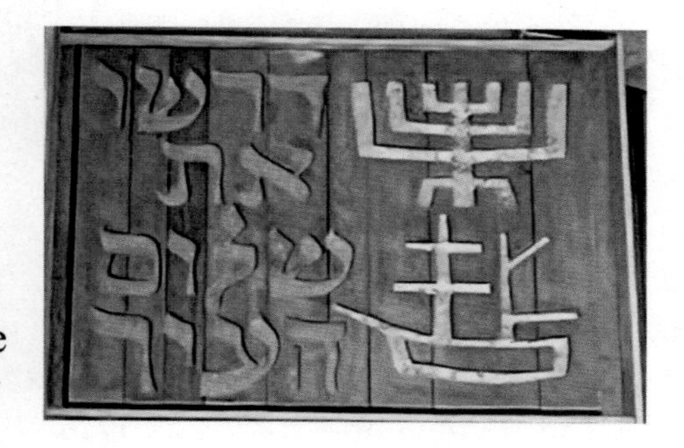

The 1968 Temple dedication booklet and a 1981 visitor's guide both contain more complete explanations of the panels' symbolism and Hebrew phrases. A recent brochure titled 'Creating Wonder' includes additional biographical information and expands on the themes of the carvings. The booklet includes full source text, including transliteration and Hebrew lettering with vowels.

## 13. **Sea Glass**

Find a pair of folding glass doors that recall a miracle.

The folding doors that enclose the Ark in the Sanctuary evoke the miracle of the parting of the Red Sea during the Exodus. Each window has a rounded top, matching the tablet shape of the Ten Commandments. The doors were sponsored by Dorothy and Phil Grenley and created in 1987 to replace fabric curtains. The Ark is situated so that worshippers face East, towards Jerusalem.

The Ark contains six Torah scrolls with hand-woven covers bearing the words of the *Sh'ma.* The covers were created through a congregational weaving project in the year 2000. Over 400 members took turns weaving threads through hand looms. Shelley Rozen led the project and completed the construction of the covers.

The hanging lamp above the Ark is the *Ner Tamid,* the Eternal Flame. The Ark is flanked by two lighted metal sculptures of seven-branched menorahs, also set on an arched background.

Two large blown-glass menorahs are situated on either side of the Sanctuary's raised platform, the *bimah*. They recall the miracle of the burning bush witnessed by Moses. The art pieces were commissioned by Babe and Herman Lehrer in 2006. They were created by glass artist Bryan Rubino for the Douglas Granum studio. A painting of the same subject is displayed just outside the Sanctuary doors.

On the north wall of the Sanctuary is a layered metal sculpture titled "Indenture," drawing on ancient financial practices from the Torah. Tom Torrens created the work in the 1980s as a memorial to the late Ruth Levy, for display in a new Davies Pearson law firm building. Decades later the Levy family donated the sculpture to Temple Beth El. The installation, spanning nearly fifteen feet, was dedicated on August 26, 2022.

## 14. **Doors that Listen**

Find the set of doors with a carving of the watchword of the Jewish faith.

The words of the *Sh'ma* (Deuteronomy 6:4) span both double doors that provide exterior access from the hallways outside the Sanctuary. The verse is carved on the outside of the painted doors facing South Vassault Street, and on the inside of the doors facing South 12th Street.

A menorah with seven branches is portrayed on the painted exterior doors on the south entrance. The ancient symbol of Judaism identified the building as a Jewish house of worship to all visitors who came through that entrance.

The double doors on the west side of the building provide egress from the hallway between the Sanctuary and the Chapel. Their carvings show the Ten Commandments as two tablets bearing the first ten letters of the Hebrew alphabet.

Are you keeping track? How many depictions of the Ten Commandments have you seen so far?

Another set is now in the conversational nook, next to several artifacts from the first Temple Beth Israel. However, these concrete tablets are from the eastern rooftop of the 1925 Talmud Torah building. They were salvaged after the synagogue building was sold in 1968. (During demolition, one of the sections slipped from the crane and the Fifth Commandment was broken off.) The artifacts were stored outside Temple Beth El for decades, then re-discovered by students and brought indoors. The support frames were fabricated by the Washington State Historical Society for a 2016 exhibit.

## 15. **1981 Biblical Garden**

Find the outdoor sculpture by the same artist as "Indenture."

"Sound the great horn for our freedom." This 1986 sculpture, inspired by the Shofar, was created by Tom Torrens. It is one of several located in the Biblical Garden, long a popular setting for Confirmation class photos.

Temple Beth El's Biblical Garden was dedicated April 19, 1981. A visitor's guide from that year noted that the garden was designed to "provide a place for quiet solitude, a place for relaxation, and a place for friends to gather while enjoying a variety of plants known to have grown on the Israeli landscape. The garden offers a contrast between the Pacific Northwest garden, with plants and granite rocks which are indigenous to our Cascade range, and the Israeli garden, with its ruins amid desert sands set with plants to be found in Israel."

Marty Lyon served as the landscape architect, Victor Lyon was chairman of the special committee, and Phil Simon was financial chairman. A gift from Bernard Brotman in memory of his wife, Pearl, was the first of many that helped make the garden possible. A more recent bench is in remembrance of Alan Warnick and John Warnick.

Other art pieces in the garden include a sundial, and a large stone sculpture inspired by Deuteronomy 34:10, "Never again did there arise in Israel a prophet like Moses."

A landscape plan and complete listing of the many plant types is displayed in a notebook in the conversation nook.

The Biblical Garden was re-dedicated in 1998 in honor of Victor and Elise Lyon and Family.

## 16. **1982 Fiber Art Tapestries**

Find the wall hangings representing twelve families.

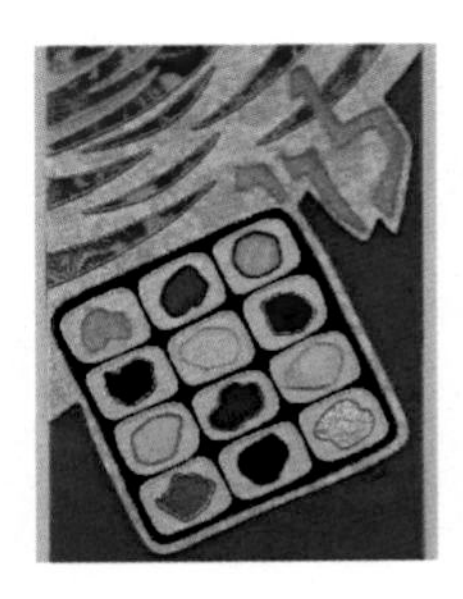

Twelve tapestries beautify the four walls of the Chapel, surrounding congregants during services. The panels represent the twelve tribes of Israelites. During the Exodus the tribes camped around the Tent of Meeting, and each displayed the banner of their ancestral house.

The tapestries are the work of fiber artist and congregant Analee Reutlinger, inspired by Marc Chagall's 1977 'America Windows' in Chicago. The banners were commissioned by Adelyn and Warren Barde, in memory of Adelyn's mother, Anna Brenner Meier Sigel, who died in 1980.

Mrs. Reutlinger encouraged members of the congregation to contribute a variety of fabrics for the project. She crafted the tapestries over a six-month period, creating two complementary panels each month. The banners were originally mounted in the main foyer below the tower glass.

The Chapel occupies a space that originally housed the Temple's library. The room now provides overflow seating during major holiday services and for many years offered an intimate space for traditional Saturday morning services. It was renamed the Rosenthal Chapel in 1997 in recognition of the 41 years of service of Barbara and Rabbi Richard Rosenthal.

The *Ner Tamid,* the Eternal Flame hanging above the small Ark, was previously in the Sanctuary of Talmud Torah/Sinai Temple. The wooden doors of the Ark bear small wooden representations of the tablets of the Ten Commandments. They were crafted in 2002 by Warren Barde, *z"l,* to cover damage from an anti-Semitic incident.

## 17. **1993 Connection in Time**

Find the timeline beginning with Abraham.

This tile recalls the very beginning of the history of the Jewish people. It is the first of a series of timeline tiles set in a stone wall, starting near the original entrance to the 1968 building. Suggested by Rabbi Rosenthal, the timeline continues up a ramp, through a 1993 addition, and along a covered exterior walkway extending to the parking lot. Visitors see the timeline in reverse, starting with the reunification of Jerusalem in 1967, and are taken back in time as they draw nearer to the Sanctuary.

Twenty-five years of growth and stability meant that by 1992 the congregation was once again running out of classroom space. The Temple board undertook a major fundraising campaign to match donors with specific needs. Architect Rodney Bauch designed an addition that included expanded offices, modern restrooms, and a large kitchen and social hall; all positioned around a central rotunda. The full 3-D model mentioned earlier was created to depict Temple Beth El with this additional wing.

The Merit Company was responsible for construction. The congregation celebrated the dedication of the new space in April 1994.

The 1968 building had been designed with three distinct areas, fulfilling the definition of the synagogue as a center of worship, a center of study, and a center of assembly and community. The 1993-1994 renovation of the Sanctuary, the center of worship, included new chandeliers, lighter woodwork on the *bima* furniture and railings, and padded fabric on the pews.

The renovation and addition doubled the classroom space, the center of study. The former reception office (now the Judaica Shop) and the rabbi's study (now the Meeting Room) were converted to classrooms. The existing social hall was transformed into a second *(Bet)* wing of classrooms, which explains why there are some awkward posts in the hallways. The former kitchen is still in use as an art room.

The addition created a new suite of office space and a large social hall and industrial kitchen: the center of assembly and community.

In 1993 the congregation also celebrated the centennial anniversary of the founding of Reform Temple Beth Israel. The cover of the banquet booklet "Centuries to Celebrate," featured a painting by Temple member Kalee Kirschenbaum.

## 18. **Repurposed Doors**

Find the carvings of the burning bush.
*(Hint – they are near a fire door.)*

This carving represents the miracle of Moses and the burning bush. It appears on the kitchen side of each of four substantial pocket doors that close the serving counter between the social hall and the kitchen. They served as the main entrance doors of the Temple until the 1993 expansion, then were cleverly repurposed.

The new kitchen was equipped with multiple prep sinks and workstations, stainless steel counters, and an industrial gas oven and cooktop. The Temple Sisterhood helped outfit the kitchen and has since routinely provided needed upgrades. Recent donations included several professional convection ovens, an industrial stand mixer, and an upright freezer.

As with many other congregations, the kitchen is the hub of activities throughout the week. On Fridays the smell of challah baking permeates the wing of the building.

Most congregants have likely never seen or noticed the carvings on the kitchen side of the doors, since they are hidden in the wall when the doorway is open. However, when the doors are closed their carvings facing the social hall combine to display a dramatic verse from the Torah.

The words are those of Jacob, from Genesis 28:17. "*Ma-nora hamakom hazeh ein zeh ki im-beit Elohim v'zeh shaar hashmayim,*" meaning "How awesome is this place! This is none other than the house of God and this is the gate to heaven!" The verse relates directly to the name of the congregation Beth El, meaning House of God.

## 19. **Courtyard Dreams**

Find a garden sculpture of someone dreaming.

This sculpture depicts Jacob dreaming of a ladder connecting heaven and earth, just before awakening and declaring, "How awesome is this place!" The installation was created by Lucille Feist Hurst, *z"l,* and is located in the courtyard outside the social hall. Nearby are five towering evergreens that symbolize the five books of the Torah.

The concrete patio of the courtyard is set with tiles bearing the names of Jewish matriarchs and patriarchs, with Abraham and Sarah in the center. It also has fixtures set in the ground for supporting the outdoor harvest shelter at Sukkot.

The recent addition of light strings overhead expands the use of the courtyard into the evening. On weekdays the fenced courtyard doubles as a preschool play area.

A legacy gift from Jeff and Susan Brotman in 2014 established the Brotman Early Learning Center. Architect Marlene Drucker supervised the major renovation, adapting the Temple's 1968 *aleph* classroom wing.

The center opened on September 8, 2015. A planned 2025 renovation will expand the facility from four classrooms to six. BELC enrolls students from age six weeks through five years and offers year-round childcare. Developmentally appropriate learning programs incorporate Jewish traditions and values.

Rabbi Keren Gorban regularly participates in programming such as reading to the students in the courtyard Sukkah.

## 20. **Perpetual Calendar**

Find the calendar that circles continually from year to year.

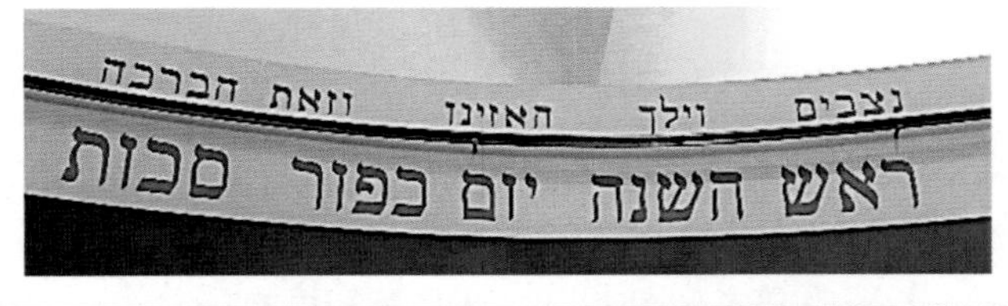

This perpetual calendar, also suggested by Rabbi Rosenthal, is painted on a soffit ledge surrounding the perimeter of the rotunda. The rotunda and calendar were key elements of the 1993 building addition.

The large Hebrew letters on the lower portion of the calendar feature major Jewish holidays throughout the year. *(Upper: Rosh Hashana, Yom Kippur, and Sukkot. Lower: Chanukah.)* The smaller Hebrew letters on the upper row of the calendar depict the names of the 54 weekly Torah portions, often taken from one of the first words of the first verse.

A brass railing circling the room carries a moveable pointer, or *yad*, indicating the current date. Each week the Rabbi physically slides the pointer to the next reading. Some feel a global connection through this calendar, as most Jews around the world read from the same portion on the same date. Others embrace the cyclical nature of reading and rereading the Torah. However, students who enter the building as they are studying for their *bar* or *bat mitzvah* are graphically reminded of the number of weeks remaining before their personal celebration day.

The rotunda now serves as a reception area from the secured main entry on the north. The large space is frequently used to stage donations of food, clothing, and school supplies for annual charity drives. These campaigns are an essential part of the Jewish value of *Tikkun Olam,* repairing the world.

A seating area on the opposite side of the rotunda provides a place for families with young children to take a break. Formerly the location of the Sisterhood Judaica Shop, the corner walls have built-in cases that offer books and display art and artifacts.

Due to its circular design, the rotunda has a special acoustical effect near the walls. Historically this benefit has purposely been employed to create a "whispering gallery." Partner with a friend and give it a try!

## 21. **History Underfoot**

Find the time capsule tucked away for future generations.

**"WHOSO KEEPS THE COMMANDMENT SHALL KNOW NO EVIL THING, AND A WISE ONE'S HEART KNOWS TIME AND JUDGEMENT."**

These words are written on a ring set in the center of a Star of David and positioned in the center of the floor of the rotunda. Underneath is a time capsule, placed by members of the congregation during the 1993 renovation and addition.

ה שׁוֹמֵ֣ר מִצְוָ֔ה לֹ֥א יֵדַ֖ע דָּבָ֣ר רָ֑ע וְעֵת֙ וּמִשְׁפָּ֔ט יֵדַ֖ע לֵ֥ב חָכָֽם׃

*Ecclesiastes 8:5*

When do you think the congregation should open the time capsule? What do you think might be inside? What items would you contribute for future generations?

# Temple Beth El Rabbis

**Rabbi Richard Rosenthal,** ***z" l*** (1929-1999)

Rabbi Rosenthal led Temple Beth Israel from August 1956 through the congregational merger in June 1960. He continued as Rabbi of Temple Beth El until his retirement in 1997 and served as Rabbi Emeritus until his death.

**Rabbi Mark Glickman** led Temple Beth El from 1997 through June 2004. As of this writing he is the spiritual leader of Temple B'nai Tikvah in Calgary, Alberta, and is a popular speaker and author.

**Rabbi Bruce Kadden** served as Temple Beth El's rabbi from July 2004 until his retirement in June 2020. He continues as Rabbi Emeritus and teaches locally.

**Rabbi Keren Gorban** joined Temple Beth El in July 2022, after serving as the Associate Rabbi of Temple Sinai in Pittsburgh for seven years.

## Additional Artwork by Congregants of Blessed Memory, *z"l*

**"Festivals"**
**Tile Mosaic**
by Berte Gollan Schneider
(1914-2012)
North wall of the
conversation nook

**"Binding of Isaac"**
**Stone Sculpture**
by Lucille Feist Hurst
(1916-2010)
East wall of the
main foyer

**"Noah's Ark"**
**Intarsia Woodwork**
by Warren Barde
(1922-2017)
Stairwell by the
Biblical Garden

**“Megillit Esther” Quilt Project**
by Barbara Binder Kadden
(1954-2018)
South wall of the social hall

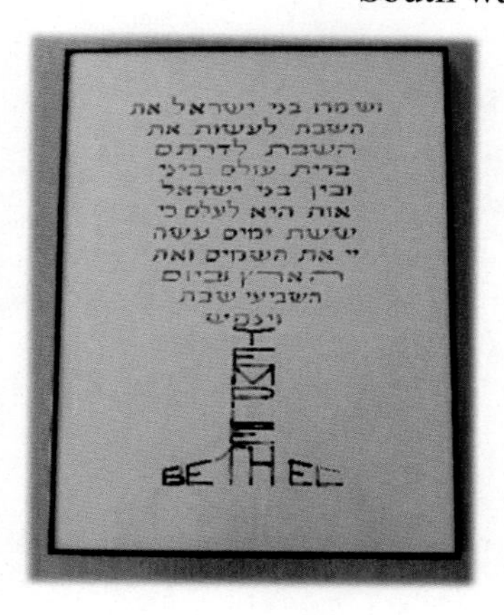


**“V’Shamru, Temple Beth El”**
by George Martin
(1913-1996)
South wall of the office

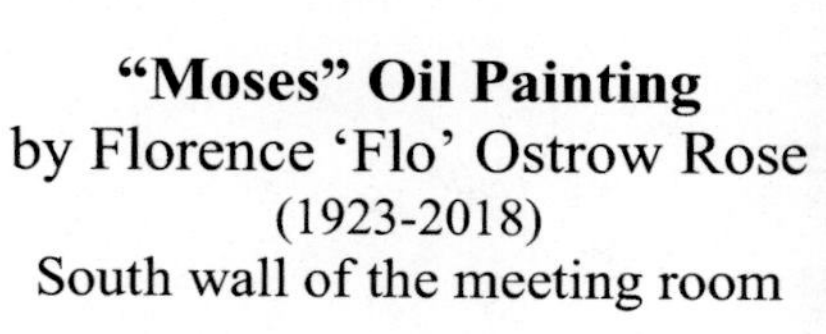

**“Moses” Oil Painting**
by Florence ‘Flo’ Ostrow Rose
(1923-2018)
South wall of the meeting room

# Memorial Window Dedications

2nd Temple Beth Israel

North 4th and J Streets

In memory of:
Meyer Kaufman (Died March 17, 1900, aged 70)
and
Flora Kaufman (Died June 17, 1886, aged 38)
By their daughter Carrie Kaufman Andrews

In memory of:
Samuel Feist (1839-1917) and Bertha Dreyfus
Parents of Theophil Feist (1873-1940)
and
Bertram Levy (1844-1900) & Lena Metzger (1859-1946)
Parents of Jessie Levy Feist (1887-1976)

In memory of:
George (abt. 1823-1893) and Bertha Klaber (1844-1911)
Parents of Herman Klaber, who died
April 14, 1912, on the *RMS Titanic*

In memory of:
Carrie Kaufman Andrews
(1875-1917)
Second wife of Samuel A. Andrews

In memory of:
Armand Wormser Jacob
(March 27, 1902-June 30, 1905)
Son of Meyer & Jennie Jacob
Grandson of Alexander Jacob & Pauline Wormser

In memory of:
David Levin
January 18, 1852-August 9, 1911
and
May Karnes Levin
March 3, 1862-September 10, 1916
By their daughter Ethel Levin Dornberg

In memory of:
Morris Bloom
June 16, 1850-March 24, 1919
By Mrs. Jennie Bloom
August 12, 1860-February 15, 1949
And children Nathan, Henry, Ella & Emma

In memory of:
Rose Schneider Friedman
March 20, 1878-June 3, 1924
Widow of Philip B Friedman
1884-1920
By her children Robert, Aaron & Samuel Thorne
Madelle and Bernice Friedman

In memory of:
Herman A. Kaufman
1865-1926
By his wife Margaret F. Kaufman (1884-1959)
And his daughter Elsa Kaufman Levinson

## Photo Permissions

Courtesy of Temple Beth El or the author,
unless otherwise noted below

**Page 5**: First Seventh Day Adventist Church building at 921-923 South I in 1931, Northwest Room at the Tacoma Public Library, Chapin Bowen Collection, TPL-6764.
**Page 6:** Julius Friedman bookplate, from his grandson, Harold Friedman. “Hebrew Orthodox” quotation from the *Tacoma Daily Ledger*, Friday, September 30, 1892.
**Page 7:** Chevra Talmud Torah 1908 Agreement to Incorporate, Washington State Archives.
**Page 12:** Talmud Torah southwest entrance July 1942, Jerry Donion Estate.
**Page 13:** Talmud Torah students in 1928, Northwest Room at the Tacoma Public Library, Boland-B-18322.
**Page 14:** Talmud Torah 1940 Confirmation Class: Rabbi Treiger, Edith Brodsky, Sylvia Friedman, Beverly Goldfarb, Adelyn Meier and Philip Simon.
**Page 17:** Richard Rosenthal oral history interview, August 24, 1989, Washington State Jewish Historical Society.
**Page 19:** *(Left)* Former Temple Beth Israel in 1977, Northwest Room at the Tacoma Public Library, BU-654. *(Right)* Sinai Temple in 1964, Northwest Room at the Tacoma Public Library, Richards D-141770-15.
**Page 20:** Extended Kleiner family at the 1967 groundbreaking, courtesy of Greg Kleiner.
**Page 21:** Temple Beth El congregation in the Sanctuary, circa 1968, Northwest Room at the Tacoma Public Library, Richards Studio D-154095-3.
**Page 23:** Harold Balazs, www.findagrave.com, Memorial ID 187442790.
**Page 36:** Tapestry design copyright 1982 by Analee Reutlinger.
**Page 50:** 324 North J, Google Street View July 2012.

## Sisterhood of Temple Beth El

This book is presented as a gift to the Sisterhood of Temple Beth El, in appreciation for the hard work and leadership of Tacoma's many strong Jewish women, spanning more than a century.

### *What We're All About*

**On a personal level**, for decades, Sisterhood of Temple Beth El in Tacoma has been a group of women who have formed lifelong bonds by empowering ourselves to run a Jewish organization, not just a committee of the Board of TBE.

**On a local level**, we are dedicated to the education and enhancement of Temple Beth El families. We bring people together to form a community and provide ways for adults and youth to connect more to Judaism and its tenets.

**On a larger scale**, we are a branch of Women of Reform Judaism (WRJ) that strengthens the voice of women worldwide, empowers caring communities, nurtures congregations, cultivates personal and spiritual growth, and advocates for and promotes progressive Jewish values.

As always, we are
Stronger Together!

# Twenty-One Tales

Earlier titles in this series, published by Tacoma Historical Society:

- Tacoma's Twenty-One Tales Every Student Should be Able to Tell *(2010)*
- Rising Up from Tacoma's Twenty-One Disasters and Defeats *(2015)*
- Speaking Out: Twenty-One of Tacoma's Social Justice and Civil Rights Champions *(2018)*
- Leading Ladies: Twenty-One of Tacoma's Women of Destiny *(2019)*
- Sounds of Our City: Twenty-One Musical Tales from Tacoma History *(2021)*

Other titles by the author, writing as Deborah K. Freedman:

- Tacoma's Dry Goods and Wet Goods: Nineteenth Century Jewish Pioneers *(2016)*
- Bank on Tacoma: 1893 to 1993 *(2020)*

With co-author Harold Friedman:

- Tacoma's Shul: Talmud Torah-Sinai Temple *(2022)*
- Tacoma's Reform Congregation Temple Beth Israel: 1892 to 1960 *(2023)*

Made in the USA
Middletown, DE
13 January 2025